The Future of Media E[...]
Platforms and [...]

Gabriel Gaudi

Copyright © [2023]

Title: The Future of Media Embracing Electronic Platforms and Technologies

Author's: Gabriel Gaudi.

All rights reserved. No part of this publication may be reproduced, stored in a retrieval system, or transmitted in any form or by any means, electronic, mechanical, photocopying, recording, or otherwise, without the prior written permission of the publisher or author, except in the case of brief quotations embodied in critical reviews and certain other non-commercial uses permitted by copyright law.

This book was printed and published by [Publisher's: Gabriel Gaudi] in [2023]

ISBN:

TABLE OF CONTENTS

Chapter 1: Introduction to Electronic Media   06
The Evolution of Media

Understanding Electronic Platforms and Technologies

Chapter 2: The Impact of Electronic Media on Traditional Media   10
Disruption of Print Media

Transformation of Broadcasting

Challenges and Opportunities for Traditional Media

Chapter 3: Exploring Electronic Platforms and Technologies   16
Social Media: A New Era of Communication

Mobile Applications and Their Influence

Online Streaming: The Future of Entertainment

Chapter 4: The Role of Artificial Intelligence in Media   22
Machine Learning in Content Creation

Personalized Recommendations and Targeted Advertisements

Chatbots and Virtual Assistants in Customer Engagement

Chapter 5: The Future of Journalism in the Digital Age 28

Citizen Journalism and User-Generated Content

Data Journalism: Unleashing the Power of Big Data

Ethics and Challenges of Digital Journalism

Chapter 6: The Transformation of Advertising and Marketing through Electronic Media 34

Digital Advertising: From Pop-ups to Native Ads

Influencer Marketing and Brand Collaborations

Data-Driven Marketing Strategies

Chapter 7: The Impact of Electronic Media on Entertainment and Content Consumption 40

Streaming Services: The New Era of Television

Virtual Reality and Augmented Reality in Gaming and Film

Transmedia Storytelling: Engaging Audiences Across Multiple Platforms

Chapter 8: The Future of Media Regulation and Policy in the Digital World 46

Balancing Freedom of Expression and Content Moderation

Copyright and Intellectual Property in the Digital Age

Government Surveillance and User Privacy

Chapter 9: The Influence of Electronic Media on Society and Culture   52

Social Media and its Effects on Relationships and Mental Health

Digital Divide: Access and Inequality in the Digital World

The Rise of Fake News and Disinformation

Chapter 10: Embracing the Future: Strategies for Media Organizations   58

Investing in Technological Innovations and Infrastructure

Harnessing Data Analytics for Audience Insights

Collaboration and Partnerships in the Digital Ecosystem

Conclusion: Embracing the Electronic Future of Media   64

Chapter 1: Introduction to Electronic Media

The Evolution of Media

In an era defined by technological advancements and rapid digitalization, the landscape of media has undergone a remarkable transformation. This subchapter explores the evolution of media, with a particular focus on electronic platforms and technologies that have revolutionized the industry.

The advent of electronic media marked a turning point in the way information was disseminated, consumed, and shared. From the introduction of radio and television to the rise of the internet and social media, electronic platforms have played a pivotal role in shaping the media landscape.

One of the earliest electronic media forms was radio, which allowed for the broadcast of news, entertainment, and music to a wide audience. This innovation revolutionized the way information was delivered, eliminating the need for physical distribution and enabling real-time communication across vast distances. The subsequent introduction of television further expanded the reach of electronic media, providing a visual medium that captivated audiences worldwide.

However, the true revolution occurred with the rise of the internet. The internet not only facilitated the dissemination of information but also transformed the media landscape into an interactive and participatory space. The emergence of websites, blogs, and online news outlets blurred the lines between consumers and producers, empowering individuals to create and share content on a global scale.

In recent years, social media platforms have taken center stage, enabling users to connect and engage with content in ways never before imagined. The rise of platforms like Facebook, Twitter, and Instagram has given individuals a voice and transformed the way news is consumed. These platforms have also presented new challenges for traditional media outlets, as the line between news and opinion becomes increasingly blurred.

Furthermore, the evolution of media has witnessed the convergence of different forms of electronic media. Today, smartphones and tablets have become the primary means of accessing news and entertainment, consolidating various media forms into a single device. This convergence has brought about new opportunities for content creators while presenting challenges for traditional media outlets to adapt and remain relevant in a rapidly changing landscape.

As we look to the future, the evolution of media shows no signs of slowing down. Emerging technologies such as virtual reality, artificial intelligence, and blockchain are poised to further transform the industry, offering new ways to consume and interact with media content.

In conclusion, the evolution of media has been marked by the rapid development of electronic platforms and technologies. From radio and television to the internet and social media, these innovations have fundamentally transformed the media landscape, empowering individuals and presenting new challenges for traditional outlets. As we embrace the future of media, it is crucial for media professionals to adapt and harness the power of electronic platforms and technologies to thrive in an ever-evolving industry.

Understanding Electronic Platforms and Technologies

In today's rapidly evolving media landscape, electronic platforms and technologies have completely transformed the way we consume and engage with media content. From streaming services and social media platforms to virtual reality and artificial intelligence, these electronic advancements have revolutionized the media industry, offering new opportunities and challenges for both media professionals and consumers.

Electronic platforms refer to the digital spaces where media content is created, distributed, and consumed. These platforms have enabled a democratization of media production, allowing anyone with an internet connection to become a content creator and share their work with a global audience. Social media platforms like Facebook, Twitter, and Instagram have become powerful tools for individuals and businesses to connect with their audiences, build communities, and promote their brands. Additionally, streaming platforms such as Netflix, Hulu, and Spotify have disrupted traditional distribution models, providing consumers with on-demand access to a vast array of entertainment options.

Technologies like virtual reality (VR) and augmented reality (AR) have also made significant strides in the media industry. VR allows users to immerse themselves in virtual environments, offering new possibilities for storytelling and creating truly immersive experiences. AR, on the other hand, overlays digital information onto the real world, enhancing the user's perception and interaction with their surroundings. These technologies have the potential to revolutionize entertainment, marketing, and even education, providing unique and engaging experiences for audiences.

Artificial intelligence (AI) has emerged as another game-changer in the media industry. AI-powered algorithms can analyze vast amounts of data to provide personalized recommendations, improving user experience on platforms like YouTube, Netflix, and Amazon. AI also plays a crucial role in content creation, with some news organizations using AI to generate news articles and virtual anchors delivering real-time news updates.

However, as we embrace these electronic platforms and technologies, it is important to consider the potential challenges they bring. Issues such as data privacy, misinformation, and algorithmic bias have raised concerns about the impact of electronic media on society. Media professionals and consumers must actively engage in critical thinking and media literacy to navigate this digital landscape responsibly.

In conclusion, electronic platforms and technologies have revolutionized the media industry, offering new opportunities for content creation, distribution, and consumption. From social media platforms to virtual reality and artificial intelligence, these advancements have transformed the way we connect, engage, and interact with media content. As media professionals and consumers, it is essential to understand and embrace these electronic platforms and technologies while also being aware of the challenges they present. By doing so, we can navigate this ever-changing media landscape and harness the full potential of electronic media for the future.

Chapter 2: The Impact of Electronic Media on Traditional Media

Disruption of Print Media

In the rapidly evolving landscape of media, one cannot ignore the profound impact of electronic platforms and technologies on traditional print media. The rise of digitalization has disrupted the once-dominant print industry, challenging its conventions, business models, and even the way information is consumed by audiences. This subchapter explores the disruption of print media, discussing the factors behind its decline, the consequences for the industry, and the opportunities that arise from this transformation.

The digital revolution has unleashed a series of technological advancements that have revolutionized the media landscape. The widespread adoption of electronic devices such as smartphones, tablets, and e-readers has made information readily accessible to consumers, anytime and anywhere. This accessibility, coupled with the convenience of digital platforms, has significantly impacted the traditional print media industry, leading to a decline in circulation and advertising revenues.

The shift from print to electronic media has also altered the way audiences consume news and entertainment. With the advent of social media and online news platforms, news consumption has become more personalized, interactive, and instantaneous. Users can tailor their news feeds, engage with content through comments and shares, and receive real-time updates on their preferred topics. This shift has created new challenges for traditional print media, as they struggle to compete with the immediacy and interactivity offered by electronic platforms.

The disruption of print media has also created a ripple effect on the industry's business models. With declining revenues from print advertising, media organizations have had to adapt and diversify their revenue streams. Subscription models, digital advertising, and sponsored content are just a few examples of the innovative approaches print media has taken to survive in this digital era.

Despite the challenges, the disruption of print media has also brought forth new opportunities. Electronic media platforms offer a range of possibilities for engaging audiences through multimedia storytelling, interactive features, and immersive experiences. Media organizations that embrace these technologies can create unique and engaging content that resonates with their digital-savvy audiences.

In conclusion, the disruption of print media by electronic platforms and technologies has brought about significant changes for the industry. The decline of print circulation, the transformation of news consumption habits, and the need for innovative business models have all challenged traditional print media. However, this disruption also presents new opportunities for media organizations to embrace the digital revolution, redefine their strategies, and create compelling content for their audiences. By leveraging electronic platforms and technologies, media professionals can navigate this changing landscape and stay relevant in the future of media.

Transformation of Broadcasting

The Transformation of Broadcasting

In the digital age, the broadcasting industry has undergone a remarkable transformation, revolutionizing the way we consume media. This subchapter will explore the significant changes that have shaped the landscape of broadcasting and how electronic platforms and technologies have played a crucial role in this evolution.

Gone are the days when we relied solely on traditional television and radio broadcasts for our news, entertainment, and information. The rise of electronic media has brought about a paradigm shift, empowering individuals with the ability to access content anytime, anywhere. The internet has become a powerful medium, enabling broadcasters to reach a global audience with ease.

One of the most notable transformations in broadcasting is the shift towards on-demand content. Streaming platforms like Netflix, Hulu, and Amazon Prime Video have disrupted traditional broadcasting models by offering viewers the freedom to choose what they want to watch and when they want to watch it. This has challenged the notion of appointment viewing, allowing consumers to personalize their media consumption experience.

Furthermore, social media platforms have become an integral part of broadcasting, facilitating the sharing and dissemination of content. With the rise of platforms like YouTube, TikTok, and Instagram, individuals can now create and share their own content, blurring the line between consumer and producer. This democratization of broadcasting has given rise to a new wave of influencers and content creators who have gained immense popularity and influence.

The emergence of mobile technology has also played a significant role in the transformation of broadcasting. Smartphones and tablets have become ubiquitous, providing users with instant access to a vast array of content. Broadcasting companies have adapted to this trend by developing dedicated apps and mobile-friendly websites, ensuring that their content is easily accessible on the go.

Furthermore, technological advancements such as high-definition (HD) and 4K resolution have enhanced the viewing experience, making broadcasts more immersive and visually captivating. Virtual reality (VR) and augmented reality (AR) technologies have also begun to make their mark in broadcasting, offering viewers a more interactive and engaging experience.

As the broadcasting industry continues to evolve, it is crucial for media professionals to embrace electronic platforms and technologies to stay relevant. The future of broadcasting lies in the seamless integration of traditional and electronic media, leveraging the power of technology to deliver content that is personalized, interactive, and immersive.

In conclusion, the transformation of broadcasting has been driven by the advent of electronic platforms and technologies. From on-demand content to social media integration and mobile accessibility, these advancements have reshaped the way we consume media. As the industry continues to evolve, embracing these new platforms and technologies will be paramount for media professionals to thrive in the digital age.

Challenges and Opportunities for Traditional Media

In the ever-evolving landscape of media, traditional media outlets are facing a multitude of challenges and opportunities brought forth by the rise of electronic platforms and technologies. This subchapter explores the shifting dynamics within the media industry, focusing on the challenges traditional media faces and the opportunities that lie ahead.

One of the foremost challenges for traditional media is the declining audience and revenue. With the proliferation of electronic media, audiences are increasingly turning to online platforms for news, entertainment, and information. This shift has led to a decline in advertising revenue for traditional media outlets, forcing them to rethink their business models and find new ways to attract and engage audiences.

Another significant challenge is the rapid pace of technological advancements. Electronic media platforms are constantly evolving, providing innovative ways to consume content and engage with audiences. Traditional media outlets must adapt to these changes and incorporate new technologies to remain relevant and competitive in the digital age. This includes embracing social media, mobile applications, and other electronic platforms to reach and interact with their target audience.

However, amidst these challenges, there are also numerous opportunities for traditional media to thrive in the digital era. One opportunity lies in the creation of multimedia content. Traditional media outlets have the advantage of having established credibility and expertise in journalism. By combining their traditional strengths with electronic platforms, they can create compelling multimedia content that engages audiences across various channels.

Additionally, traditional media can leverage the power of data analytics to gain insights into audience preferences, behaviors, and trends. This data-driven approach allows media outlets to personalize content, deliver targeted advertising, and enhance the overall user experience. By harnessing the potential of data, traditional media can regain their competitive edge in the electronic media landscape.

Furthermore, traditional media can foster collaborations and partnerships with electronic media platforms. By joining forces with popular online platforms, traditional media outlets can extend their reach, tap into new audiences, and benefit from the technological expertise of electronic media companies. This collaboration can result in innovative content distribution models and revenue-sharing opportunities.

In conclusion, traditional media faces significant challenges in the digital age, including declining audience and revenue. However, by embracing electronic platforms and technologies, traditional media outlets can transform these challenges into opportunities. By adapting their business models, incorporating new technologies, creating multimedia content, leveraging data analytics, and fostering collaborations, traditional media can thrive in the dynamic landscape of electronic media.

Chapter 3: Exploring Electronic Platforms and Technologies

Social Media: A New Era of Communication

In today's digital age, social media has revolutionized the way we communicate and interact with one another. With the advent of electronic platforms and technologies, the media landscape has undergone a significant transformation. Social media, in particular, has emerged as a powerful tool that connects people from all corners of the globe, breaking down barriers and fostering a sense of community like never before.

The rise of social media platforms such as Facebook, Twitter, Instagram, and LinkedIn has given individuals and organizations a new medium through which they can express themselves, share information, and engage with a wide audience. Electronic media, encompassing television, radio, and the internet, has found a new ally in social media, as these platforms have become an integral part of people's daily lives.

One of the key aspects of social media is its ability to facilitate real-time communication. Unlike traditional media channels, where information is disseminated in a one-way manner, social media allows for instant feedback and interaction. Through comments, likes, shares, and direct messages, users can engage in conversations, express their opinions, and connect with others who share similar interests.

Furthermore, social media has democratized the media landscape, giving a voice to individuals who were previously marginalized or unheard. With just a smartphone and an internet connection, anyone can become a content creator, sharing their stories, experiences, and perspectives with the world. This has led to the rise of citizen journalism, where ordinary people can report on events as they unfold, providing a different angle to traditional news coverage.

In addition to democratizing the media, social media has also transformed the way businesses and organizations communicate with their target audience. Brands can now directly engage with their customers, build relationships, and gather valuable insights through social media channels. This direct line of communication has opened up new opportunities for marketing and advertising, allowing businesses to reach a wider audience and tailor their messages to specific niches.

However, as social media continues to reshape the media landscape, it also raises concerns regarding privacy, fake news, and the spread of misinformation. It is crucial for media professionals in the electronic media niche to navigate these challenges and ensure that ethical standards are upheld.

In conclusion, social media has ushered in a new era of communication in the media industry. Electronic media professionals must embrace these electronic platforms and technologies to harness their full potential. By understanding the power and impact of social media, media practitioners can leverage these platforms to create meaningful connections, engage with audiences, and shape the future of media.

Mobile Applications and Their Influence

In today's digital era, mobile applications have revolutionized the way we consume and interact with media. With the increasing ubiquity of smartphones and tablets, mobile apps have become an integral part of our daily lives, transforming the landscape of electronic media. This subchapter explores the profound influence that mobile applications have had on the media industry and the way we engage with content.

Mobile applications have opened up a whole new realm of possibilities for media organizations. They have become vital tools for delivering news, entertainment, and other forms of content directly to users' fingertips. With the ability to personalize and tailor content to individual preferences, these apps have created a more engaging and immersive experience for users. Whether it's streaming movies and TV shows, listening to podcasts, or reading articles, mobile apps have made it easier than ever to access and enjoy media content on the go.

Furthermore, mobile applications have transformed the way media organizations communicate and connect with their audiences. Through interactive features like push notifications and real-time updates, apps enable media outlets to deliver breaking news and updates directly to users' devices. This instant and personalized communication fosters a stronger relationship between media organizations and their audiences, enhancing user engagement and loyalty.

The influence of mobile applications extends beyond content consumption. They have also revolutionized the way media is created and distributed. With the rise of user-generated content, apps have empowered individuals to become content creators in their own right. From vlogging to podcasting, mobile apps have democratized the media landscape, allowing anyone with a smartphone to share their stories and perspectives with the world.

Moreover, mobile applications have disrupted traditional advertising models. Through targeted advertisements and sponsored content, apps have provided new revenue streams for media organizations. By leveraging user data and preferences, these apps offer more effective and relevant advertising opportunities, ensuring a higher return on investment for advertisers.

However, as mobile applications continue to shape the future of media, challenges arise. The need for data privacy and security becomes paramount, as apps collect vast amounts of user information. Additionally, the dominance of certain apps in the market can lead to concerns around media monopolies and limited diversity of content.

In conclusion, mobile applications have had a profound influence on the media industry, transforming the way we consume, create, and interact with content. As the future of electronic media continues to evolve, mobile apps will undoubtedly play a pivotal role in shaping the media landscape, offering new opportunities and challenges for media organizations and audiences alike.

Online Streaming: The Future of Entertainment

In recent years, the advent of online streaming has revolutionized the entertainment industry, reshaping the way we consume media. This subchapter will delve into the significance of online streaming, highlighting its impact on the future of entertainment. With a specific focus on electronic media, we will explore the various aspects of this emerging trend.

Online streaming has transformed the way we access and consume content. Gone are the days when we had to rely on traditional television schedules or physical media to enjoy our favorite movies, TV shows, or music. The rise of streaming platforms such as Netflix, Hulu, and Spotify has provided us with unprecedented convenience and accessibility. With just a few clicks, we can now access a vast library of content, tailored to our individual preferences, anytime and anywhere.

One of the key advantages of online streaming is its ability to cater to niche audiences. Unlike traditional broadcast media, which often targets a broad demographic, streaming platforms offer a wide range of content catering to specific interests. This has given rise to a flourishing electronic media niche, where enthusiasts can explore and immerse themselves in content that aligns with their passions. From gaming channels on Twitch to music playlists on Spotify, online streaming has created a diverse ecosystem that caters to the unique preferences of electronic media consumers.

Furthermore, online streaming has democratized media production and distribution. In the past, the entertainment industry was primarily controlled by a few major players, limiting the opportunities for independent creators to showcase their work. However, with the rise of platforms like YouTube and TikTok, anyone with a creative vision and internet connection can now produce and distribute their content to a global audience. This has not only given rise to a new wave of content creators but has also allowed for more diverse and inclusive stories to be told.

The future of entertainment undoubtedly lies in the realm of online streaming. As technology continues to advance, we can expect further innovations in streaming platforms, creating more immersive and interactive experiences for consumers. From virtual reality to augmented reality, the possibilities are endless. The convenience, personalization, and democratization offered by online streaming have transformed the media landscape, making it an essential aspect of electronic media and opening up new avenues for content creators and consumers alike.

In conclusion, online streaming has revolutionized the entertainment industry and is poised to shape the future of electronic media. Its ability to cater to niche audiences, democratize content production, and provide unparalleled convenience has made it an indispensable part of our lives. As we embrace electronic platforms and technologies, it is crucial for media professionals and enthusiasts to understand the potential and significance of online streaming in order to stay ahead in this rapidly evolving landscape.

Chapter 4: The Role of Artificial Intelligence in Media

Machine Learning in Content Creation

In recent years, the field of media has experienced a rapid transformation with the advent of electronic platforms and technologies. One of the most intriguing developments in this realm is the integration of machine learning into content creation processes. Machine learning, a subset of artificial intelligence, enables electronic media professionals to streamline and enhance their production workflows, resulting in more engaging and personalized content.

At its core, machine learning involves training algorithms to analyze large volumes of data and make predictions or decisions without explicit programming. This technology has revolutionized various industries, and the media sector is no exception. By harnessing the power of machine learning, media professionals can optimize content creation processes in several ways.

Firstly, machine learning algorithms can analyze vast amounts of data to identify patterns and trends, helping media practitioners gain insights into audience behavior and preferences. This information is invaluable for creating content that resonates with target audiences, ultimately leading to higher engagement and loyalty. By understanding what types of content are more likely to captivate viewers, media professionals can tailor their creations to meet specific niche interests within the electronic media landscape.

Furthermore, machine learning can facilitate the automation of certain content creation tasks. For instance, algorithms can generate storylines, scripts, or even entire articles based on predefined criteria or templates. This automation not only saves time and resources but also allows media professionals to focus on more creative and strategic aspects of content development, thereby enhancing overall quality.

Additionally, machine learning algorithms can personalize content delivery. By analyzing user data, including browsing history, preferences, and demographics, these algorithms can recommend tailored content to individual viewers. This personalized approach can significantly enhance user experience, increasing the likelihood of continued engagement and loyalty. Moreover, by leveraging machine learning, media professionals can optimize content distribution, ensuring that the right content reaches the right audience at the right time.

However, it is important to note that while machine learning offers significant opportunities for content creation, human creativity and intuition remain essential. Machine learning is a tool that can augment and enhance the creative process, but it cannot replace the unique perspectives and ideas that humans bring to the table.

In conclusion, the integration of machine learning into content creation processes has the potential to revolutionize the electronic media landscape. By leveraging this technology, media professionals can gain valuable insights into audience preferences, automate certain tasks, and personalize content delivery. However, it is crucial to maintain a balance between the power of machine learning and human creativity to ensure the production of engaging and impactful content in the future.

Personalized Recommendations and Targeted Advertisements

In today's fast-paced world of electronic media, personalized recommendations and targeted advertisements have become an integral part of our daily lives. As media consumers, we are constantly bombarded with a vast amount of content and information, making it increasingly challenging to navigate through the digital landscape. However, thanks to advancements in technology and data analytics, personalized recommendations and targeted advertisements have emerged as powerful tools that not only enhance our media consumption experience but also provide immense benefits to businesses.

Personalized recommendations utilize algorithms and machine learning techniques to analyze user behavior and preferences, allowing media platforms to deliver content tailored to individual interests. Whether it's streaming services recommending movies and TV shows based on our viewing history or music platforms suggesting songs based on our listening habits, these personalized recommendations have revolutionized the way we discover and engage with media content. By curating content specifically for each user, media platforms are able to create a more immersive and satisfying experience, ultimately increasing user engagement and retention.

Targeted advertisements, on the other hand, leverage the vast amount of data collected from users to deliver highly relevant and personalized advertisements. Gone are the days of generic advertisements that appeal to a broad audience. With targeted advertisements, businesses can now reach their desired niche audience more effectively, resulting in higher conversion rates and return on investment. By analyzing user demographics, browsing history, and online behavior, advertisers can segment their audience and deliver advertisements that align with their interests and preferences. This not only benefits businesses by increasing their chances of reaching the right audience but also benefits consumers by exposing them to advertisements that are more likely to be of interest to them.

While personalized recommendations and targeted advertisements offer numerous advantages, they also raise concerns about privacy and data security. As media consumers, it is crucial for us to be aware of the data we provide to these platforms and understand how it is being used. Media platforms must prioritize the security and privacy of user data, ensuring that it is collected and utilized in a responsible and transparent manner.

In conclusion, personalized recommendations and targeted advertisements have transformed the landscape of electronic media. By tailoring content and advertisements to individual interests and preferences, media platforms are able to provide a more engaging and relevant experience for users. However, it is essential that both media platforms and consumers remain vigilant about data privacy and security to ensure a mutually beneficial relationship between personalized recommendations, targeted advertisements, and users.

Chatbots and Virtual Assistants in Customer Engagement

In today's ever-evolving digital landscape, customer engagement has become a crucial aspect of media strategies, particularly in the realm of electronic media. With the rise of chatbots and virtual assistants, businesses are presented with new opportunities to connect with their audience in a more personalized and efficient manner. This subchapter explores the role of chatbots and virtual assistants in customer engagement and highlights their significance in the future of electronic media.

Chatbots, powered by artificial intelligence, have revolutionized customer interactions by providing instant responses and assistance. They are computer programs designed to simulate human conversation through text or voice-based communication. By leveraging natural language processing and machine learning algorithms, chatbots can understand and respond to customer queries, provide recommendations, and even make transactions on behalf of the user. These intelligent bots can be integrated into various electronic media channels, including websites, social media platforms, and messaging applications, allowing businesses to engage with their customers in real-time and on their preferred platforms.

Virtual assistants, on the other hand, take chatbot technology to the next level by incorporating voice recognition capabilities. These voice-enabled assistants, such as Amazon's Alexa, Apple's Siri, or Google Assistant, have gained immense popularity due to their convenience and ease of use. By simply speaking commands or asking questions, users can access a wide range of services, including media content, weather updates, and even make purchases. Virtual assistants have become an integral part of many households, bridging the gap between consumers and electronic media platforms.

The integration of chatbots and virtual assistants in customer engagement has several benefits for both businesses and consumers. Firstly, they provide round-the-clock customer support, ensuring that queries are addressed promptly, even outside of business hours. This enhances customer satisfaction and loyalty, as users feel valued and supported. Moreover, chatbots and virtual assistants enable businesses to gather valuable data and insights about their customers' preferences, behaviors, and pain points. This information can be leveraged to personalize content, recommendations, and offers, thus enhancing the overall customer experience.

As electronic media continues to evolve, chatbots and virtual assistants will play an increasingly vital role in customer engagement. Their ability to offer personalized interactions, instant responses, and seamless experiences make them indispensable tools for businesses looking to stay competitive in the digital age. By embracing these technologies, electronic media can foster stronger relationships with their audience, deepen customer loyalty, and drive business growth in the future.

Chapter 5: The Future of Journalism in the Digital Age

Citizen Journalism and User-Generated Content

In today's digital era, the landscape of media is rapidly evolving, and traditional journalism is no longer the sole source of news and information. The rise of electronic platforms and technologies has given birth to a new phenomenon known as citizen journalism. This subchapter explores the concept of citizen journalism and the impact of user-generated content on the future of media.

Citizen journalism refers to the practice of ordinary individuals, often with no formal training in journalism, engaging in reporting, analyzing, and disseminating news and information. With the advent of social media platforms and the widespread availability of smartphones, anyone with access to the internet can now become a citizen journalist. This democratization of news production has led to a significant shift in the media landscape, empowering individuals to participate actively in the creation and distribution of news content.

One of the key aspects of citizen journalism is user-generated content (UGC). UGC refers to any form of content, including text, images, and videos, that is created by users rather than professional journalists or media organizations. The proliferation of UGC has transformed the way news is consumed, as people now rely on social media platforms and online communities to stay informed.

The rise of citizen journalism and UGC has both positive and negative implications for the future of media. On the positive side, citizen journalism provides increased diversity and plurality of perspectives. It allows for the coverage of local events and issues that may not receive attention from mainstream media outlets. Additionally, citizen journalists often have direct access to situations that professional journalists may not be able to reach, resulting in real-time reporting and immediate updates.

However, the influx of citizen journalism and UGC also raises concerns regarding the credibility and reliability of information. Unlike professional journalists, citizen journalists may lack the necessary training and ethical guidelines, leading to the spread of misinformation and fake news. Media consumers must be critical and discerning in evaluating the credibility of sources and information in this new digital landscape.

The future of media lies in embracing electronic platforms and technologies while finding a balance between professional journalism and citizen journalism. Media organizations need to adapt their business models to incorporate UGC while upholding journalistic standards and verifying information. Collaboration between professional journalists and citizen journalists can lead to a more comprehensive and diverse media ecosystem.

In conclusion, citizen journalism and user-generated content are reshaping the media landscape. While it offers new opportunities for participation and diversity, it also presents challenges in terms of credibility and quality. As media consumers, it is crucial to navigate this evolving landscape with critical thinking and media literacy, ensuring that the future of media is built on a foundation of reliable and trustworthy information.

Data Journalism: Unleashing the Power of Big Data

In today's fast-paced world, where information is readily available at our fingertips, media organizations are constantly seeking innovative ways to capture the attention of their audience. One such avenue that has emerged in recent years is data journalism. This subchapter explores the potential of data journalism and how it harnesses the power of big data to create impactful stories in the realm of electronic media.

The rise of electronic platforms and technologies has revolutionized the way we consume news. With an overwhelming amount of data being generated every second, it has become crucial for journalists to sift through this vast sea of information to uncover meaningful insights. This is where data journalism comes into play. By leveraging big data analytics, journalists are able to unearth patterns, trends, and connections that were previously hidden from plain sight.

One of the key advantages of data journalism in the electronic media niche is its ability to provide a visual representation of complex issues. Through the use of interactive charts, graphs, and maps, data journalists can break down intricate data sets into digestible formats. This not only enhances the audience's understanding but also engages them on a deeper level, making the news more relatable and accessible.

Furthermore, data journalism enables media organizations to uncover stories that might have otherwise gone unnoticed. By analyzing large datasets, journalists can identify social, economic, and political trends that impact our society. Whether it is uncovering corruption scandals, exposing social injustices, or tracking the spread of infectious diseases, data journalism has the potential to shed light on critical issues and hold those in power accountable.

However, data journalism also presents challenges that need to be addressed. Journalists must possess the necessary skills to analyze and interpret complex data sets accurately. Additionally, ethical concerns surrounding data privacy and security must be carefully navigated to ensure responsible journalism practices.

As the future of media continues to embrace electronic platforms and technologies, data journalism will play an increasingly vital role. Media organizations need to invest in training their journalists in data analysis techniques and data visualization tools. By doing so, they can unlock the immense potential of big data and deliver impactful stories that resonate with their audience.

In conclusion, data journalism is a powerful tool that empowers media organizations to harness the potential of big data. Through the use of electronic platforms and technologies, journalists can uncover hidden stories, provide visual representations of complex issues, and engage their audience on a deeper level. As the future of media unfolds, embracing data journalism will be essential in delivering accurate, insightful, and impactful news in the electronic media niche.

Ethics and Challenges of Digital Journalism

Title: Ethics and Challenges of Digital Journalism

Introduction:
In today's rapidly evolving media landscape, the rise of electronic platforms and technologies has revolutionized journalism, presenting both exciting opportunities and daunting challenges. As digital journalism continues to shape the way information is produced, disseminated, and consumed, it is imperative for media professionals, particularly those in electronic media, to navigate the ethical dilemmas and obstacles that come with this new era. This subchapter explores the ethics and challenges of digital journalism, providing insights and guidance for media practitioners.

1. Ethics in the Digital Age:
Digital journalism brings forth a unique set of ethical considerations. From issues surrounding accuracy, verification, and source attribution to privacy concerns, media professionals must grapple with maintaining credibility and upholding ethical standards in an era of instant information sharing and social media influence. This section delves into key ethical principles and provides strategies for practitioners to navigate the digital landscape responsibly.

2. Misinformation and Fake News:
One of the biggest challenges of digital journalism is combating misinformation and fake news. With the ease of content creation and dissemination, false narratives can spread rapidly, eroding public trust in media. This section explores the impact of misinformation, the ethical responsibilities of journalists in countering it, and the strategies they can employ to verify information and promote accuracy in their reporting.

3. Digital Security and Privacy: Digital journalism raises significant concerns about the security and privacy of both journalists and their sources. As electronic media professionals embrace digital platforms, they must understand the potential risks involved, such as hacking, data breaches, and surveillance. This section highlights the importance of secure communication channels, the ethical implications of protecting sources, and strategies for safeguarding privacy in the digital realm.

4. Transparency and Accountability: The digital era calls for increased transparency and accountability in journalism. This section discusses the importance of disclosing conflicts of interest, affiliations, and financial influences to maintain public trust. It also explores the challenges of holding powerful entities accountable in the digital realm, such as social media platforms and tech giants, and the ethical considerations involved in investigative reporting.

Conclusion:

As electronic media professionals, embracing digital platforms and technologies presents exciting opportunities to engage audiences and shape the future of journalism. However, it also demands a commitment to ethical practices and an awareness of the challenges that lie ahead. By addressing the ethics and challenges of digital journalism head-on, media practitioners can navigate this ever-evolving landscape with integrity, ensuring that journalism remains a trusted source of information in the digital age.

Chapter 6: The Transformation of Advertising and Marketing through Electronic Media

Digital Advertising: From Pop-ups to Native Ads

In today's fast-paced and interconnected world, electronic media plays a pivotal role in shaping the way we consume information and engage with brands. As the digital landscape continues to evolve, so does the realm of advertising. In this subchapter, we will explore the transformation of digital advertising from intrusive pop-ups to the rise of native ads, revolutionizing the way brands connect with their audience.

Pop-up ads, once a common sight on almost every website, have garnered a reputation for being disruptive and annoying. They often interrupted the user's browsing experience, leading to frustration and a decline in user engagement. However, the ever-growing demand for more effective and less intrusive advertising strategies has paved the way for the emergence of native ads.

Native advertising seamlessly integrates with the surrounding content, creating a more organic and engaging experience for the audience. These ads blend in with the platform they are displayed on, making them appear as if they are part of the original content. By aligning with the style and tone of the platform, native ads effectively capture the attention of the audience without being obtrusive.

One of the key advantages of native advertising is its ability to provide relevant and valuable content to the user. Unlike traditional ads, native ads offer informative and entertaining content that aligns with the interests and preferences of the target audience. By providing value rather than interruption, brands can build trust and establish a stronger connection with their customers.

Furthermore, native ads are highly adaptable and can be tailored to suit various platforms and devices. With the proliferation of smartphones and tablets, advertisers have recognized the need to optimize their content for mobile consumption. Native ads allow brands to seamlessly integrate their messages across different devices, ensuring a consistent and engaging experience for the user.

As digital advertising continues to evolve, it is crucial for media professionals to stay abreast of the latest trends and technologies. By embracing native advertising, brands can effectively cut through the noise and capture the attention of their target audience. This subchapter serves as a guide for media professionals in understanding the shift from pop-up ads to native ads and how they can leverage this transformative approach to enhance their digital advertising strategies.

In conclusion, the shift from pop-ups to native ads represents a significant milestone in the evolution of digital advertising. By providing a more seamless and engaging user experience, native ads offer a way for brands to connect with their audience in a more meaningful and impactful manner. As the future of media embraces electronic platforms and technologies, it is imperative for media professionals to embrace the power of native advertising to drive success in the digital realm.

Influencer Marketing and Brand Collaborations

The digital revolution has transformed the media landscape and given rise to new opportunities for brands to connect with their target audiences. One of the most effective strategies in this new era is influencer marketing and brand collaborations. In this subchapter, we will explore how electronic media has played a significant role in shaping this trend and discuss its implications for the future of media.

Influencer marketing refers to the practice of partnering with individuals who have a significant following and influence on social media platforms. These influencers, often known as content creators, have established trust and credibility with their audience, making them valuable partners for brands looking to tap into niche markets. By collaborating with influencers, brands can leverage their reach and engagement to create authentic, relevant, and compelling content that resonates with their target audience.

The rise of electronic media platforms, such as social media networks and video-sharing sites, has provided a fertile ground for influencer marketing to thrive. These platforms have democratized content creation and distribution, allowing anyone with a smartphone and internet access to become a content creator. As a result, a diverse range of influencers has emerged, catering to niche interests and passions.

Electronic media has also enabled brands to measure the effectiveness of influencer marketing campaigns more accurately. Through advanced analytics and tracking tools, brands can now quantify the reach, engagement, and conversions generated by their collaborations with influencers. This data-driven approach allows brands to optimize their strategies, identify the most effective influencers, and allocate their resources more efficiently.

However, the evolving landscape of influencer marketing and brand collaborations also presents challenges. As the market becomes saturated with influencers, it becomes crucial for brands to identify the right partners who align with their values and objectives. Authenticity and transparency are key factors in successful collaborations, as audiences are increasingly demanding genuine connections and honest recommendations.

Furthermore, as influencer marketing becomes more prevalent, regulators and consumers are scrutinizing the space for potential ethical concerns, such as undisclosed sponsorships or deceptive practices. Brands must navigate these challenges carefully to maintain trust and credibility with their audience.

In conclusion, influencer marketing and brand collaborations have become integral components of the media ecosystem, particularly in the realm of electronic media. By partnering with influencers, brands can leverage their reach and credibility to create meaningful connections with their target audience. However, brands must also navigate the challenges of authenticity, transparency, and ethical considerations to ensure long-term success in this evolving landscape. The future of media undoubtedly lies in embracing electronic platforms and technologies, and influencer marketing is at the forefront of this exciting transition.

Data-Driven Marketing Strategies

In today's digital landscape, data-driven marketing strategies have become a critical component for anyone involved in the media industry, particularly within the niche of electronic media. The ability to harness the power of data and leverage it effectively can make all the difference in staying ahead of the competition and engaging with target audiences in a meaningful way.

Data-driven marketing involves the collection, analysis, and interpretation of vast amounts of data to inform decision-making and shape marketing strategies. The advent of electronic platforms and technologies has provided media professionals with an unprecedented ability to access and utilize data in ways that were unimaginable just a few years ago.

One of the primary benefits of data-driven marketing strategies is the ability to gain valuable insights into consumer behavior. By tracking and analyzing consumer data, media organizations can better understand their audience's preferences, interests, and needs. This knowledge enables them to tailor their content, advertising, and marketing messages to resonate with their target demographic, increasing the likelihood of engagement and conversion.

Another advantage of data-driven marketing is the ability to measure the effectiveness of campaigns and initiatives. By monitoring key performance indicators (KPIs) such as click-through rates, conversion rates, and engagement metrics, media professionals can gauge the success of their marketing efforts in real-time. This allows for quick adjustments and optimizations to maximize results and return on investment.

Furthermore, data-driven marketing strategies enable media organizations to personalize and customize their offerings. By analyzing individual consumer data, media professionals can deliver highly targeted and relevant content and advertisements. This level of personalization not only enhances the user experience but also increases the likelihood of creating long-term customer loyalty.

However, it is important for media professionals to approach data-driven marketing ethically and responsibly. Privacy concerns and data protection regulations require media organizations to handle consumer data with utmost care and transparency. Building trust with their audience is crucial, and maintaining data privacy and security is a fundamental aspect of this trust-building process.

In conclusion, data-driven marketing strategies are revolutionizing the media industry, particularly within the realm of electronic media. By harnessing the power of data, media professionals can gain valuable insights, measure campaign effectiveness, personalize offerings, and ultimately, engage with their audience in a more impactful and meaningful way. Embracing data-driven marketing is no longer an option but a necessity for media organizations looking to thrive in this rapidly evolving digital landscape.

Chapter 7: The Impact of Electronic Media on Entertainment and Content Consumption

Streaming Services: The New Era of Television

The landscape of television has experienced a seismic shift in recent years with the rise of streaming services. Traditional television is being challenged by digital platforms that offer on-demand content, giving viewers greater control and flexibility over their entertainment choices. In this subchapter, we explore the emergence of streaming services and their impact on the future of television.

Streaming services, such as Netflix, Hulu, and Amazon Prime Video, have revolutionized the way we consume media. Gone are the days of waiting for a specific time slot to catch our favorite shows or relying on reruns. With streaming, viewers can access a vast library of content at any time, on any device, and from anywhere with an internet connection.

One of the key advantages of streaming services is the ability to binge-watch entire seasons or series in one sitting. This has led to a shift in storytelling, as creators can develop narratives that are meant to be consumed in one go, rather than stretched out over weeks or months. This new approach to storytelling has captivated audiences and created a cultural phenomenon around shows like "Stranger Things" and "The Crown."

Additionally, streaming services have opened doors for niche and independent content that may not have found a place on traditional television networks. These platforms allow for greater diversity and experimentation in storytelling, giving underrepresented voices a chance to be heard. As a result, we are witnessing a renaissance in television, with innovative shows pushing the boundaries of what is possible.

The rise of streaming services has also disrupted the traditional advertising model. With the option to subscribe to ad-free services, viewers are becoming less tolerant of interruptions during their viewing experience. This has forced advertisers to find new ways to reach audiences, such as product placement and branded content. As the industry continues to evolve, advertisers and content creators will need to adapt to these changing dynamics.

However, streaming services are not without their challenges. The increasing number of platforms and subscriptions can become overwhelming for consumers, leading to subscription fatigue. Additionally, the sheer volume of content available can make it difficult for new shows to stand out and gain traction.

In conclusion, streaming services have ushered in a new era of television, empowering viewers and reshaping the industry. As traditional television continues to adapt to this digital disruption, it is crucial for media professionals in the electronic media niche to embrace these electronic platforms and technologies. The future of television lies in the hands of streaming services, and those who can navigate this new landscape will be at the forefront of the industry's evolution.

Virtual Reality and Augmented Reality in Gaming and Film

In recent years, the world of media has witnessed a revolution in the form of virtual reality (VR) and augmented reality (AR) technologies. These cutting-edge innovations have not only transformed the way we experience entertainment but have also opened up new possibilities for storytelling and immersive experiences. This subchapter explores the impact of VR and AR in gaming and film, shedding light on their potential and implications for the future of electronic media.

Gaming has always been at the forefront of technological advancements, and the integration of VR and AR has taken it to new heights. Virtual reality gaming offers players an unparalleled level of immersion, transporting them to virtual worlds where they can interact with their surroundings and characters in ways never before possible. With the help of specialized headsets and controllers, gamers can physically engage with the virtual environment, creating a sense of presence and realism that traditional gaming simply cannot replicate. From first-person shooters to puzzle-solving adventures, VR gaming has revolutionized the way we play and consume interactive content.

Similarly, augmented reality has made its mark in the gaming industry by blending the real world with digital elements. Using smartphones or specialized AR glasses, players can overlay virtual objects onto their physical environment, allowing for a seamless integration of digital content into the real world. This technology has been leveraged in popular games such as Pokémon Go, where players can capture virtual creatures in their everyday surroundings. AR gaming has the potential to transform the way we perceive and interact with our surroundings, creating a new dimension of gameplay that blurs the line between fantasy and reality.

Beyond gaming, VR and AR have also found their place in the world of film and storytelling. Virtual reality films provide viewers with a fully immersive and sensory experience, allowing them to step into the narrative and become active participants. Directors and content creators now have the ability to craft stories that not only captivate audiences but also enable them to explore and navigate the narrative at their own pace. From documentaries that transport viewers to far-flung places to fictional narratives that allow them to inhabit the bodies of characters, VR films offer a new level of engagement and intimacy that traditional cinema cannot replicate.

Augmented reality, on the other hand, has the potential to enhance the cinematic experience by overlaying digital elements onto the real world. Imagine watching a film on your smartphone or AR glasses and seeing additional information or graphics pop up on the screen, enriching the narrative and providing a deeper understanding of the story. This technology has the power to revolutionize the way we consume and engage with films, making them more interactive and immersive.

In conclusion, virtual reality and augmented reality have revolutionized the gaming and film industries, offering unprecedented levels of immersion and interactivity. These technologies have the potential to reshape the way we consume and engage with electronic media. Gamers can now step into virtual worlds and interact with their surroundings, while film enthusiasts can immerse themselves in narratives through VR experiences or enhance their viewing with augmented reality elements. As electronic media continues to evolve, virtual reality and augmented reality are at the forefront, pushing the boundaries of storytelling and entertainment.

Transmedia Storytelling: Engaging Audiences Across Multiple Platforms

In today's rapidly evolving media landscape, traditional forms of storytelling are giving way to a more immersive and interactive approach known as transmedia storytelling. This innovative technique allows creators to engage audiences across multiple platforms, such as television, film, video games, social media, and more. Transmedia storytelling has become increasingly popular in the realm of electronic media, captivating audiences and providing a richer, more dynamic narrative experience.

One of the key advantages of transmedia storytelling is its ability to immerse audiences in a multi-dimensional world. By extending a story across various platforms, creators can deepen the narrative, introduce new characters and plotlines, and foster a sense of interactivity. For example, a television series may be supplemented by a mobile game that allows viewers to further explore the show's universe, interact with characters, and even influence the storyline. This level of engagement not only captivates audiences but also keeps them coming back for more.

Moreover, transmedia storytelling enables creators to target niche audiences within the broader media landscape. With electronic media, it becomes easier to reach specific demographic groups or cater to niche interests. By leveraging different platforms, creators can tailor their content to specific audience preferences, ensuring a more personalized and engaging experience. This approach not only increases audience satisfaction but also opens up new revenue streams by tapping into niche markets.

In addition, transmedia storytelling encourages active participation from audiences. Through social media platforms, viewers can share their thoughts, theories, and feelings about the story, sparking discussions and creating a sense of community. This interactive element not only enhances the audience's connection to the narrative but also provides valuable feedback for creators, helping them refine and improve their content.

However, while transmedia storytelling offers exciting opportunities, it also poses unique challenges. Creators must carefully balance consistency and coherence across different platforms, ensuring that each piece of the narrative contributes to the overall story while being accessible on its own. Additionally, the rapid pace of technological advancements requires creators to stay adaptable and embrace emerging platforms and technologies to keep the audience engaged.

In conclusion, transmedia storytelling has emerged as a powerful tool in the realm of electronic media. By engaging audiences across multiple platforms, creators can create a more immersive, interactive, and personalized narrative experience. As the future of media continues to embrace electronic platforms and technologies, transmedia storytelling will undoubtedly play a crucial role in captivating audiences and driving innovation within the industry.

Chapter 8: The Future of Media Regulation and Policy in the Digital World

Balancing Freedom of Expression and Content Moderation

In today's digital era, where electronic media platforms have become the primary means of communication, the question of balancing freedom of expression and content moderation has become increasingly complex and crucial. As media professionals, it is imperative for us to understand the delicate equilibrium between these two fundamental aspects of the digital landscape.

Freedom of expression is a cornerstone of any democratic society, allowing individuals to voice their opinions, share information, and participate in public discourse. Electronic media platforms have revolutionized the way people exercise this right, providing a global stage for diverse viewpoints and empowering individuals to become content creators. However, this freedom is not without its challenges.

The exponential growth of electronic media has led to an overwhelming volume of content being generated and shared daily. With this abundance of information, the need for content moderation arises. Content moderation ensures that the content disseminated on these platforms adheres to certain guidelines and standards, protecting users from harmful or offensive material. It also helps maintain the credibility and integrity of the platforms themselves.

However, striking a balance between freedom of expression and content moderation is no easy task. On one hand, excessive content moderation can lead to the suppression of legitimate voices and stifle creativity. It may also enable censorship, limiting the diversity of narratives and perspectives available to the public. Such restrictions

Copyright and Intellectual Property in the Digital Age

In today's rapidly evolving digital landscape, the issue of copyright and intellectual property has become more complex than ever before. As society increasingly relies on electronic media, it is crucial to understand the implications and challenges that arise in protecting creative works in this digital age.

The emergence of electronic media has brought remarkable benefits, including the ease of sharing information and the democratization of creativity. However, it has also posed significant challenges to copyright holders, as digital content can be easily reproduced, distributed, and manipulated without permission. This has led to widespread copyright infringement and piracy, resulting in substantial financial losses for creators and rights holders.

The concept of intellectual property encompasses a wide range of creative works, including music, films, books, software, and art. In the digital age, protecting these works has become increasingly challenging. With the advent of file-sharing platforms, social media, and streaming services, unauthorized distribution and consumption of copyrighted content have become effortless. This has prompted the need for new strategies and technologies to safeguard intellectual property in the digital realm.

Digital rights management (DRM) has emerged as a popular solution to combat online piracy. DRM technologies aim to control access to digital content, preventing unauthorized copying and distribution. However, DRM has faced criticism for its potential negative impact on user experience and fair use rights. Striking a balance between protecting copyright and allowing legitimate uses of digital content remains a complex challenge.

can undermine the principles of free speech and hinder democratic discourse.

On the other hand, an absence of content moderation can result in the proliferation of harmful content, including hate speech, misinformation, and cyberbullying. This can have severe consequences, both individually and collectively. The responsibility lies with media professionals and electronic media platforms to develop effective content moderation strategies that maintain a safe and inclusive digital environment while respecting the principles of free expression.

The future of media lies in striking a delicate balance between these two seemingly contradictory elements. It requires the collaboration and cooperation of media professionals, electronic media platforms, and policymakers to establish clear guidelines and frameworks for content moderation. Transparency and accountability are crucial in ensuring that the moderation process is fair, unbiased, and in line with societal norms.

By embracing this challenge and finding innovative solutions, we can create a future where freedom of expression thrives alongside responsible content moderation. It is only through this delicate balance that electronic media platforms can continue to empower individuals, foster democratic dialogue, and shape the future of media in a positive and inclusive manner.

The rise of user-generated content platforms has further complicated the copyright landscape. Platforms such as YouTube and TikTok enable individuals to create and share their own content, often incorporating copyrighted material without permission. This has raised questions about the boundaries of fair use and the responsibility of platforms in regulating copyright infringement.

To address these issues, policymakers and industry stakeholders have been working to update copyright laws and establish clearer guidelines for digital content. Copyright infringement lawsuits and legal battles have become more prevalent, leading to significant changes in legislation and court rulings.

In conclusion, the digital age has presented both opportunities and challenges for copyright and intellectual property protection. As electronic media continues to shape our society, it is essential for stakeholders, including creators, consumers, and platforms, to navigate the complex landscape of copyright in a way that balances the rights of creators while fostering innovation and creativity in the digital world.

Government Surveillance and User Privacy

In today's digital age, where electronic media plays a dominant role in our lives, the issue of government surveillance and user privacy has become a topic of utmost concern. As we embrace electronic platforms and technologies, it is crucial to understand the implications and potential risks associated with the collection and monitoring of personal data by governments.

Government surveillance refers to the systematic monitoring and gathering of information on individuals or groups by governmental authorities. While the intentions behind such surveillance may vary, it is essential to strike a delicate balance between national security and the protection of individual privacy rights.

One of the primary concerns surrounding government surveillance is the potential erosion of user privacy. In an era where our personal information is stored, accessed, and shared through various electronic platforms, individuals are becoming increasingly vulnerable to unwarranted intrusions into their lives. Government agencies can collect vast amounts of data, including emails, phone calls, browsing history, and even location data, without explicit consent or knowledge from users.

The implications of government surveillance on electronic media are far-reaching. For media professionals, the potential chilling effect of surveillance can hinder investigative journalism and the free flow of information. Whistleblowers and sources may be deterred from coming forward, fearing retribution or exposure. This can have serious consequences for the media's role in holding governments accountable and ensuring transparency.

Furthermore, the accumulation of personal data by governments can lead to potential abuses and breaches of privacy. The unauthorized use or sharing of this data can result in identity theft, discrimination, or manipulation of individuals for political or commercial gain. This poses a significant threat to the trust users place in electronic media platforms and technologies.

To address these concerns, it is essential for governments to establish robust legal frameworks and oversight mechanisms. Transparency regarding the extent of surveillance activities, as well as clear guidelines on data collection and retention, can help mitigate the risks and protect user privacy. Additionally, incorporating privacy-enhancing technologies and encryption measures can provide individuals with greater control over their personal information.

As media professionals and consumers, it is crucial to be aware of the potential risks associated with government surveillance and the impact it can have on user privacy. By advocating for stronger privacy protections and engaging in informed debates, we can ensure that electronic media platforms and technologies continue to evolve in a manner that respects individual rights and fosters a free and democratic society.

In conclusion, the issue of government surveillance and user privacy in the context of electronic media is a complex and multifaceted topic. As we navigate the future of media, it is imperative to strike a delicate balance between national security and the protection of individual privacy rights. By addressing these concerns head-on and advocating for stronger privacy protections, we can ensure that electronic media remains a powerful tool for communication, innovation, and democratic participation.

Chapter 9: The Influence of Electronic Media on Society and Culture

Social Media and its Effects on Relationships and Mental Health

In today's digital age, social media has become an integral part of our lives, transforming the way we communicate, interact, and consume information. Electronic media has revolutionized the way we connect with others, but it also brings along its own set of challenges. This subchapter explores the effects of social media on relationships and mental health, shedding light on both the positive and negative aspects of this technological phenomenon.

Social media platforms have undoubtedly made it easier to connect with friends, family, and even strangers from all over the world. They provide an avenue for sharing thoughts, experiences, and important life events. People can now maintain relationships even across vast distances, fostering a sense of belonging and community. Electronic media allows individuals to express themselves creatively, engage in meaningful conversations, and explore diverse perspectives.

However, it is important to acknowledge the potential negative impacts of social media on relationships and mental well-being. The constant exposure to carefully curated versions of other people's lives can lead to feelings of inadequacy, envy, and low self-esteem. The pressure to present an idealized version of oneself on social media can lead to a distorted sense of reality and contribute to the rise of anxiety and depression.

Moreover, social media can also affect the quality of our personal relationships. The overconsumption of electronic media can lead to decreased face-to-face interactions, resulting in a lack of genuine connections. People may become more reliant on virtual interactions, compromising the depth and authenticity of their relationships. The phenomenon of "phubbing" (phone snubbing) has become increasingly common, where individuals prioritize their online presence over real-time interactions, causing feelings of neglect and frustration.

To mitigate the negative effects of social media, it is crucial to develop healthy digital habits. Setting boundaries and limiting screen time can help individuals prioritize real-life connections and foster healthier relationships. Practicing mindful social media usage, such as being aware of emotional reactions to posts and taking breaks from social media, can also contribute to overall mental well-being.

In conclusion, while social media has revolutionized electronic media and brought numerous benefits, it also presents challenges that can affect relationships and mental health. Understanding the potential negative consequences of excessive social media usage is essential for both media professionals and individuals in the electronic media niche. By embracing a balanced approach and developing healthy digital habits, we can harness the positive aspects of social media while safeguarding our well-being and the quality of our relationships.

Digital Divide: Access and Inequality in the Digital World

In today's rapidly evolving world, the digital divide has become a critical issue that demands our attention. As the world becomes increasingly connected, access to electronic platforms and technologies has become a necessity, shaping the future of media. However, not everyone has equal access to these resources, leading to significant inequalities in the digital world.

The digital divide refers to the gap between those who have access to electronic media and those who do not. This divide can manifest in various forms, including access to the internet, digital devices, and technological literacy. Unfortunately, these disparities often mirror existing social and economic inequalities, exacerbating the challenges faced by marginalized communities.

Access to the internet is a fundamental aspect of the digital divide. While the majority of the world's population now has internet access, there are still significant disparities in connectivity. Many rural areas, particularly in developing countries, lack reliable internet infrastructure, limiting access to valuable information and opportunities for residents. Furthermore, socioeconomic factors can also play a role in access to the internet, as lower-income individuals may struggle to afford the necessary devices and data plans.

In addition to internet access, digital devices also contribute to the digital divide. While smartphones have become increasingly affordable, not everyone can afford the latest technology. This creates a disparity in terms of functionality and access to advanced features, limiting the opportunities available to those with older or less capable devices.

Technological literacy is another crucial aspect of the digital divide. While the younger generation often adapts quickly to new technologies, older individuals may struggle to navigate the digital world. This creates a generational gap, where the older population may be left behind in terms of accessing information, job opportunities, and social connectivity.

Addressing the digital divide requires collective effort from governments, technology companies, and society as a whole. Initiatives such as improving internet infrastructure in underserved areas, providing affordable devices, and offering digital literacy programs can bridge the gap and ensure equal access to electronic platforms and technologies.

By addressing the digital divide, we can create a more inclusive and equitable digital world. It is crucial for media professionals, particularly those in electronic media, to understand the challenges faced by marginalized communities and use their platforms to advocate for change. Embracing electronic platforms and technologies should not be limited to those who can afford it but should be a right for all individuals, regardless of their socioeconomic status. Only by closing the digital divide can we truly harness the potential of the digital world for the betterment of society.

The Rise of Fake News and Disinformation

In this digital age, the media landscape has undergone a profound transformation with the advent of electronic platforms and technologies. While these advancements have opened up new avenues for information dissemination, they have also given rise to an alarming phenomenon – the proliferation of fake news and disinformation.

Fake news refers to deliberately fabricated or misleading information that is presented as genuine news. It has become a pressing concern in recent years, as it can have far-reaching consequences on public opinion, elections, and even national security. The rise of social media platforms and the ease of sharing information have provided fertile ground for the rapid dissemination of fake news to millions of users worldwide.

Disinformation, on the other hand, encompasses a broader range of misleading or false information spread with the intention to deceive. It includes propaganda, conspiracy theories, and intentionally skewed narratives. Disinformation campaigns are often driven by political or commercial motives, aiming to manipulate public sentiment or undermine trust in established institutions.

The impact of fake news and disinformation on the media industry cannot be underestimated. Media organizations are confronted with the challenge of maintaining their credibility and relevance in an era where misinformation can spread like wildfire. The trust between media outlets and their audiences has been eroded, as the line between factual reporting and opinion has become increasingly blurred.

The electronic media, in particular, has been both a victim and perpetrator of fake news. While electronic platforms have enabled a democratization of information, they have also provided an easy breeding ground for the dissemination of false narratives. The speed at which information travels on these platforms often leaves little time for fact-checking, leading to the viral spread of unverified or misleading content.

To combat the rise of fake news and disinformation, media organizations and electronic platforms must take a proactive stance. Fact-checking initiatives, collaborative efforts, and the promotion of media literacy are crucial in restoring trust and ensuring the accuracy of information. Furthermore, regulatory measures may be necessary to hold platforms accountable for the content they host.

In conclusion, the rise of fake news and disinformation poses significant challenges to the media industry, particularly in the realm of electronic media. Media organizations and electronic platforms must work together to address this issue, safeguarding the integrity of information and rebuilding trust with their audience. Only through these collective efforts can we ensure a future where reliable and accurate news prevails in the digital age.

Chapter 10: Embracing the Future: Strategies for Media Organizations

Investing in Technological Innovations and Infrastructure

In today's rapidly evolving digital landscape, investing in technological innovations and infrastructure is crucial for the survival and success of the media industry, particularly within the niche of electronic media. As traditional media platforms decline in popularity, electronic media has emerged as a dominant force, shaping the way we consume and interact with content.

Technological innovations have revolutionized the way media is produced, distributed, and consumed. From streaming services to social media platforms, electronic media has opened up new avenues for content creation and engagement. However, to fully leverage the potential of electronic media, media organizations must invest in cutting-edge technologies and robust infrastructure.

One area where investing in technological innovations is paramount is content creation. With the rise of user-generated content and the democratization of media, media organizations must adapt to the changing landscape. By embracing emerging technologies such as virtual reality, augmented reality, and artificial intelligence, media professionals can create immersive and personalized experiences for their audiences. Investing in advanced production equipment and software allows for high-quality content creation, ensuring that media organizations stay ahead of the competition.

Furthermore, investing in infrastructure plays a vital role in meeting the demands of electronic media. As audiences increasingly consume content on multiple devices and platforms, media organizations must optimize their infrastructure to deliver seamless experiences. This includes investing in robust servers, content delivery networks, and data storage solutions. A reliable and scalable infrastructure ensures that media organizations can handle high volumes of traffic, maintain fast loading times, and provide uninterrupted streaming services.

Investing in technological innovations and infrastructure not only improves the quality and delivery of content but also enhances audience engagement and monetization opportunities. By leveraging data analytics and audience insights, media organizations can tailor their content and advertising strategies to meet the demands of their target audience. This level of personalization and targeting leads to higher engagement and conversion rates, resulting in increased revenue streams for media organizations.

In conclusion, investing in technological innovations and infrastructure is essential for media organizations operating in the electronic media niche. By embracing emerging technologies, optimizing production processes, and upgrading infrastructure, media organizations can stay relevant, deliver high-quality experiences, and drive revenue growth. The future of media lies in the hands of those who are willing to invest in the cutting-edge technologies and infrastructure that will shape the industry for years to come.

Harnessing Data Analytics for Audience Insights

In today's fast-paced digital age, the media landscape is constantly evolving, with electronic platforms and technologies playing a pivotal role. As media professionals navigate this ever-changing terrain, the ability to harness data analytics for audience insights has become essential for success. This subchapter explores the power of data analytics and its potential to revolutionize the way media professionals engage with their audiences in the realm of electronic media.

Data analytics, at its core, is the systematic analysis of raw data to uncover patterns, trends, and correlations. In the context of media, it involves collecting and analyzing vast amounts of audience data to gain valuable insights into their preferences, behaviors, and interests. By leveraging data analytics, media professionals can make well-informed decisions, tailor content, and optimize marketing strategies to meet the evolving demands of their audiences.

The electronic media landscape offers an abundance of data sources, from social media platforms and streaming services to online forums and e-commerce platforms. By tapping into these rich data streams, media professionals can gain a comprehensive understanding of their audience's demographics, content consumption patterns, and engagement levels. This knowledge enables them to develop targeted content that resonates with their audience, fostering deeper connections and increasing engagement.

One of the key benefits of data analytics in electronic media is the ability to track and measure audience interactions in real-time. With the help of advanced analytics tools, media professionals can monitor the performance of their content, identify trends, and make data-driven decisions on the go. This real-time feedback loop allows for agile content creation, ensuring that media professionals can quickly adapt their strategies to suit the ever-changing preferences of their audience.

Furthermore, data analytics can also aid in the discovery of new audience segments and niche markets. By analyzing data patterns, media professionals can identify untapped opportunities and tailor their content to reach previously underserved audiences. This not only expands their reach but also opens up new revenue streams and strengthens their position in the highly competitive electronic media landscape.

However, it is crucial to approach data analytics ethically and responsibly. Media professionals must prioritize user privacy and ensure compliance with applicable data protection regulations. Transparency and consent should be at the forefront of any data collection and analysis practices, to build trust with the audience and maintain the integrity of the media industry.

In conclusion, the integration of data analytics in electronic media holds immense potential for media professionals to gain valuable insights into their audience's preferences, behaviors, and interests. By harnessing the power of data analytics, media professionals can create targeted content, optimize marketing strategies, and unlock new growth opportunities. Embracing data-driven decision-making is crucial for media professionals to stay relevant and thrive in the rapidly evolving media landscape.

Collaboration and Partnerships in the Digital Ecosystem

In today's rapidly evolving media landscape, collaboration and partnerships have become essential for success in the digital ecosystem. As electronic media continues to dominate the media industry, understanding the power of collaboration and forming strategic partnerships has become crucial for media professionals.

The digital ecosystem offers immense opportunities for media organizations to reach a wider audience and create innovative content. However, the complexity of the digital landscape requires collaboration between different media entities to leverage their strengths and resources.

Collaboration in the digital ecosystem can take various forms. Media organizations can collaborate with technology companies to develop cutting-edge platforms and tools that enhance the delivery of content. By partnering with tech giants, media companies can access the latest technologies, such as artificial intelligence and virtual reality, to create immersive and engaging experiences for their audience.

Furthermore, collaboration between media organizations themselves can lead to the creation of unique and diverse content. By pooling their expertise and resources, media entities can produce high-quality multimedia projects that cater to the evolving preferences of audiences. This collaborative approach not only increases the reach of the content but also fosters innovation and creativity within the industry.

Partnerships are equally important in the digital ecosystem. Media organizations can form strategic alliances with brands and advertisers to create mutually beneficial relationships. By partnering with brands, media companies can access additional funding and resources to produce high-quality content. On the other hand, brands can leverage the media organization's reach and influence to promote their products or services effectively.

Furthermore, partnerships with influencers and content creators can help media organizations tap into niche markets and expand their audience base. Influencers have a loyal following and can provide valuable insights into the preferences and trends of their specific niche. By collaborating with influencers, media companies can create targeted content that resonates with their audience and drives engagement.

In conclusion, collaboration and partnerships are integral to thrive in the digital ecosystem of electronic media. Media organizations must actively seek out partnerships with technology companies, brands, influencers, and content creators to leverage their strengths and resources. By embracing collaboration, media professionals can create innovative and diverse content, expand their reach, and stay ahead in this fast-paced digital landscape. The future of media lies in the power of collaboration and partnerships, and those who embrace it will undoubtedly excel in the ever-evolving electronic media industry.

Conclusion: Embracing the Electronic Future of Media

In today's fast-paced digital age, it is evident that the future of media lies in embracing electronic platforms and technologies. The rapid advancements in electronic media have revolutionized the way we consume and interact with content, presenting endless opportunities for media professionals and enthusiasts alike.

The transformative power of electronic media cannot be overstated. From the rise of social media platforms to the proliferation of streaming services, electronic media has fundamentally changed how we access news, entertainment, and information. It has enabled us to connect with a global audience in real-time, breaking down geographical barriers and fostering a sense of community like never before.

One of the key advantages of electronic media is its unparalleled accessibility. With just a few clicks or taps, individuals can access an infinite amount of content from the comfort of their own homes or on the go. This accessibility has democratized the media landscape, allowing anyone with a smartphone or computer to become a content creator and share their perspectives with the world. It has given a voice to marginalized communities and facilitated the sharing of diverse stories, ultimately enriching our collective cultural tapestry.

Furthermore, electronic media has also revolutionized the advertising industry. Traditional media channels such as television and print have been supplemented, if not replaced, by targeted online advertising. With the ability to track user data and tailor advertisements based on individual preferences, electronic media offers unparalleled opportunities for brands to reach their target audiences with precision and efficiency.

However, embracing the electronic future of media also presents challenges and ethical considerations. The proliferation of fake news and the erosion of trust in traditional journalism are among the pressing issues that need to be addressed. As media professionals, it is our responsibility to uphold journalistic integrity, fact-check information, and promote critical thinking among audiences.

In conclusion, the future of media lies in wholeheartedly embracing electronic platforms and technologies. The opportunities presented by electronic media are undeniable, as it has revolutionized accessibility, fostered global connections, and transformed the advertising industry. However, as we navigate this electronic future, it is crucial for media professionals to remain vigilant in upholding ethical standards and fostering a media landscape that is responsible, diverse, and inclusive. By harnessing the power of electronic media while being mindful of its challenges, we can shape a future where media serves as a force for positive change.

Milton Keynes UK
Ingram Content Group UK Ltd.
UKHW020232301123
433483UK00016B/968